KU-477-361

LEARNING
TO BE WILD

LEARNING TO BE WILD

Raising Orphan Grizzlies

CHARLIE RUSSELL
AND MAUREEN ENNS

HUTCHINSON
London

First published in Great Britain by Hutchinson in 2003

1 3 5 7 9 10 8 6 4 2

Text copyright © 2003 Charlie Russell

Except where noted, all photographs by Maureen Enns and Charlie Russell

Photography copyright © Charlie Russell Photography

Photography copyright © Maureen Enns Studio Ltd.

Charlie Russell and Maureen Enns have asserted their right under the Copyright, Designs and Patents Act, 1988 to be identified as the authors of this work

This book is sold subject to the condition that it shall not, by way of trade or otherwise, be lent, resold, hired out, or otherwise circulated without the publisher's prior consent in any form of binding or cover other than that in which it is published and without a similar condition including this condition being imposed on the subsequent purchaser

Published by arrangement with Random House of Canada Limited

Hutchinson
The Random House Group Limited
20 Vauxhall Bridge Road, London SW1V 2SA

Random House Australia (Pty) Limited
20 Alfred Street, Milsons Point, Sydney
New South Wales 2061, Australia

Random House New Zealand Limited
18 Poland Road, Glenfield
Auckland 10, New Zealand

Random House (Pty) Limited
Endulini, 5a Jublilee Road
Parktown 2193, South Africa

The Random House Group Limited Reg. No. 954009

www.randomhouse.co.uk

A CIP catalogue record for this book is available from the British Library

Papers used by Random House are natural, recyclable products made from wood grown in sustainable forests. The manufacturing processes conform to the environmental regulations of the country of origin

Typeset by Daniel Cullen
Printed and bound in Belgium

ISBN 0 09 179982 1

Contents

Introduction 1

Discovering Kamchatka 9

Our First Year with the Cubs 35

Learning to Be Wild 73

Strong and Independent 99

A Protocol for Co-existence between Grizzlies and Humans 151

Acknowledgements 152

Introduction

I can't imagine a world without bears. For the past seven years my partner and I have been privileged enough to live for five months of the year in a remote wood-frame cabin we built in the South Kamchatka Sanctuary, Siberia. This varied and beautiful landscape is home to the world's densest concentration of brown bears, formidable creatures who travel well-worn paths through the tundra from their winter dens down to crystal-clear waters that will become rich with spawning salmon.

For myself, a naturalist and guide born on a ranch in Alberta, I've spent over forty years studying the nature of bears and our human reponses to them. I have had the great fortune to have been joined in this, my life's work, by Maureen Enns, an artist and photographer. Maureen's first feelings were similar to those of most people, who feel fear and apprehension in the face of these giant, mysterious animals. But luckily, Maureen is the kind of creative, curious person who knows that understanding is the most important step towards conquering fear.

What Maureen and I felt instinctively was that bears were not as dangerous and unpredictable as their reputation suggested. We felt that a great part of the problem has been that, ever since humans became organized enough to do such things, grizzlies have been managed, almost exclusively, in a way that assumes these characteristics are absolute. In a sense, bears and people have been deliberately trained to fear each other, in order to keep them a safe distance apart. This policy has been particularly troublesome for bears, because grizzlies and humans both need the same type of productive land—and the grizzly most often loses in competition for it.

We thought it would be helpful for bears if we did a study that would question the central assumptions about them. Whatever a grizzly is up to, its actions are considered threatening to humans who encounter them. But many years of watching them had suggested to us that they might really be peaceful animals, not vicious predators. That they occasionally strike out could in fact be a result of incessant human reactions to them based on fear. It is surely true

Photo: Igor Revenko

that whenever such an attack occurs, it keeps paranoia simmering and reinforces the perception that bears are menacing by nature. Perhaps if bears were treated kindly, their responses to humans would be entirely different, and the cycle of violence could be broken.

Our study would differ from other biological studies, in that it would assume that these animals were intelligent and could have feelings similar to ours. Unlike scientists, we didn't feel we had to justify this approach or worry whether our findings could be viewed as objective; we would simply see where it led. Beyond pepper spray—a well-tested and non-fatal means of deterring bears—and electric fencing, the only protection we would take with us was our combined experience and understanding of our subjects.

First, we had to find a place to conduct our study. In 1993 we began researching locations, and knew it was critical to locate a large chunk of wilderness where there were many grizzly bears that had had little, if any, contact with people. Our assumption was that all previous human contact with grizzlies, world-over, would have been in some way negative for the

bears—we wanted to start with a clean slate. We also had to find a place where we'd be allowed to befriend them. Due to the concerns of wildlife officials, this requirement pretty well ruled out working in North America.

Coincidentally, the Soviet era had recently ended and less-populated areas of Russia were opening up to foreign visitors. Kamchatka Peninsula in the far east of Russia had been a particularly restricted place during the Cold War, due to its many military bases and its proximity to Alaska. Kamchatka was a majestic wilderness loaded with Asian brown bears, the same species as North America's grizzly, and a study based there would be applicable to bears at home in Canada, as well as to bears in Alaska and the rest of the United States. In the summer of 1994, we ventured into the area to scout it out. While the Russian authorities had many well-defined and negative pre-conceptions concerning the questions we were asking about bears, we nevertheless managed, after a year and a half of negotiations, to secure permission to work in their country.

Kambalnoye Lake, where we've lived for the past seven summers, is at the very bottom end of the peninsula, in the South Kamchatka

Photo of Russian sable: Alexey Maslov

Sanctuary, and is one of the last great wildernesses in the world. We have never fully understood why we have been tolerated by our Russian hosts as long as we have in this strange and distant country, but the seventh year of our study has proven more enlightening than we had ever dared to hope.

We came to understand that the bears in our study area, whom we hoped would be innocent, in actuality had had encounters with poachers over the years, so they were very fearful of us at first. But they soon began to relax when they saw that we were not overly interfering with their lives. We never allowed ourselves to make mistakes, such as letting them into our food, because living well together required being hassle-free both ways.

In our second year in Russia, our project became meaningful in a whole new way: we were able to rescue three very small orphaned cubs from a zoo and bring them to our cabin, where we looked after them until they could be on their own. Since then we have remained a part of their lives. It was the first time such rehabilitation had been done successfully, that is, without the bears becoming dangerous to humans. Our work with the cubs has been—and

still is—the most critical focus of our study, and has hastened the process of our understanding the subtleties of the true nature of grizzlies.

Typically, as our study progresses, we identify more questions needing answers. For instance, having to feed our cubs when they were young meant we were led into the thorny debate surrounding the issue. It is widely assumed that "a fed bear is a dead bear," meaning that every bear that tastes human food becomes obnoxious. But we discovered it is possible to feed bears without them becoming dangerous, if it is done in a systematic and careful way. More work must be done in this area, but often bears starve from natural food failures, and hundreds could be saved by knowing how to feed them in an appropriate manner.

With the success of the cub reintroduction project, we've also recognized the importance of ensuring that the South Kamchatka Sanctuary remains a safe habitat for bears. It's wonderful to experience the bears' openness to our presence, but unless we are able to change human attitudes, our work cannot be considered complete. Our presence in the sanctuary has discouraged much of the poaching that was happening prior to our arrival, but we worry that when we complete our project, our study

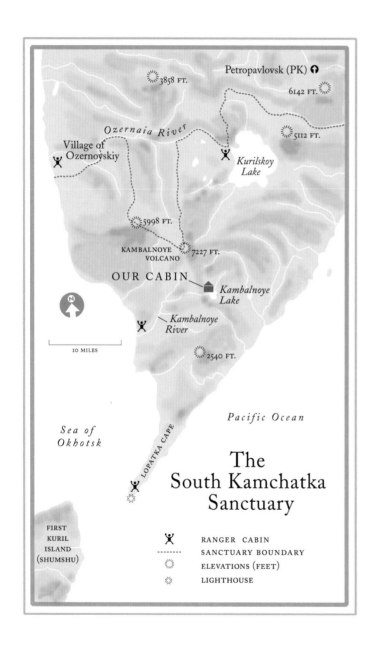

The South Kamchatka Sanctuary

Petropavlovsk (PK)

3858 FT.

6142 FT.

Ozernaia River

5112 FT.

Village of Ozernovskiy

Kurilskoy Lake

5998 FT.

KAMBALNOYE VOLCANO 7227 FT.

OUR CABIN

Kambalnoye Lake

Kambalnoye River

2540 FT.

N

10 MILES

Pacific Ocean

Sea of Okhotsk

LOPATKA CAPE

FIRST KURIL ISLAND (SHUMSHU)

✖ RANGER CABIN

⋯ SANCTUARY BOUNDARY

☼ ELEVATIONS (FEET)

☀ LIGHTHOUSE

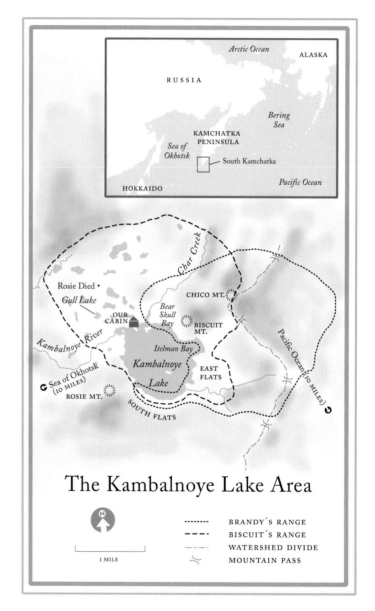

Arctic Ocean ALASKA

RUSSIA

Bering Sea

KAMCHATKA PENINSULA

Sea of Okhotsk

South Kamchatka

HOKKAIDO *Pacific Ocean*

The Kambalnoye Lake Area

Char Creek

Rosie Died

Gull Lake

CHICO MT.

Bear Skull Bay

BISCUIT MT.

OUR CABIN

Kambalnoye River

Itelman Bay

Kambalnoye Lake

EAST FLATS

Pacific Ocean (10 MILES)

Sea of Okhotsk (10 MILES)

ROSIE MT.

SOUTH FLATS

N

1 MILE

⋯ BRANDY'S RANGE

--- BISCUIT'S RANGE

–·– WATERSHED DIVIDE

)(MOUNTAIN PASS

animals will be vulnerable again. We've vowed not to leave before more protection is in place, and for the last four years we have worked with Kronotskiy State Preserve to develop the area's first ranger system. And to ensure the preserve has the resources to support such programs, we have funded the training of ecotourism guides in Canada, with hopes that the Russian people will learn how to capitalize on their incredible wilderness areas without destroying them.

We believe that grizzlies have been misunderstood. Our most important discovery is that grizzly bears respond very quickly and positively to being treated with respect. Once we understood the manners we needed to have, their world very suddenly opened for us. The many hundreds of hours we've spent in very close proximity to dozens of different bears, often with our backs turned to them, has shown us that grizzlies cannot be inherently dangerous and unpredictable. If they were, we simply would not have survived our first season. We have never suffered any injury beyond a few small scratches received while playing with our cubs, and we have yet to use our pepper spray to defend ourselves.

We hope the message people get from this book is that grizzlies can be pleasant animals, with whom it is feasible for humans to be more generous and sharing in terms of land. Our photographs demonstrate what is possible under the ideal conditions we created around our cabin, but our actions should not be imitated, for the simple reason that present management policies have ensured that most bears living near populated areas have the potential to be very dangerous. No one should ever have to repeat the type of study we have done at Kambalnoye Lake, providing we have achieved our goals. Hopefully, we have revealed that there is another way to relate to these awesome animals. With luck, we've also shown that fear is the most crippling obstruction to exploration—not only fear of the grizzly, but also fear of trying something new. The question remains whether entrenched human behaviour and beliefs can change quickly enough to make a difference.

Discovering Kamchatka 1994-1996

We first travelled to the province of Kamchatka in the summer of 1994, with only a vague idea of what we would find there, and we were dazzled by what a precious jewel it was. The place was virtually unknown, even by Russians, and had been almost entirely protected by its remoteness. There are no roads or railways joining Petropavlovsk, Kamchatka's one city, with the rest of Russia.

The most startling of the region's features are its two hundred volcanoes, many of which are active. One of these, the Kluchevskoy Volcano, rises 15,600 feet above sea level, and is the highest active volcano in Eurasia. Lush greenness, highlighted with colourful washes of wildflowers, carpets the mountainsides. The clear rivers are so full of salmon it looks as if you could walk on top of them to get across. And everywhere you look are Asian brown bears, stuffing themselves on an incredible variety of foods, including salmon.

The only way to travel the whole of Kamchatka is by helicopter, which we did, from one end of the thousand-mile-long province to the other. Away from the city, we learned these were difficult, almost desperate times. The Soviet Union had only recently broken up and social conditions were changing quickly—and not always for the better. Most governmental jobs in Kamchatka, including those with the military, had vanished, and when the value of the ruble tumbled many citizens were left destitute. These people had to find new ways to live, and the Southeast Asia bear-gall trade was one of the very few sources of income available to them. A poacher we befriended calculated that from his fishing village alone, he and four others had killed a thousand bears in three years. The poacher even agreed with us: the bears could not possibly survive such pressure for long.

When we visited Kurilskoy Lake in the south, we discovered that the situation there was not as grim. The lake was located within the South Kamchatka Sanctuary, a somewhat protected zone dedicated to wildlife preservation

A summer evening at Kurilskoy Lake.

The shore of Kurilskoy Lake is a major thoroughfare for bears. By sitting quietly, one can observe a lot of bear behaviour in a very short time.

Here, a young bear gets too close to a cranky female at the mouth of one of the many salmon streams. Spurts of sand—appearing to be standing straight up—show the high speed at which the bears are moving.

As seen from our porch, fog pours over the divide from the east, signalling a coming storm.

and scientific research. There were some signs of poaching, but the area appeared to be a bears' paradise in comparison to sites farther north. In one afternoon alone, we watched fifty bears fishing for salmon. In the evenings, after we too had stuffed ourselves with salmon, we huddled around the campfire talking to Igor Revenko, a biologist studying bears in the sanctuary. After carefully considering our proposed study and its stringent site requirements, Igor suggested Kambalnoye Lake, describing it as "the forgotten place." Only twenty-five miles to the south of Kurilskoy Lake, it sounded ideal for our project: remote, undisturbed, and populated by many, many bears.

Due to bad weather, we could not visit Kambalnoye that summer, and it was not until 1996 that we finally were able to build a cabin there and begin to settle into the landscape. Amazingly, Russian officials allowed us to bring a Kolb aircraft and enjoy the extraordinary sights and freedoms flying afforded. Nothing happened for miles around our basin that we did not see happen. The views were breathtaking: Kambalnoye Volcano towered over us, and tundra plains stretched out beneath us all the way to the Sea of Okhotsk.

Igor had been right. There were bears everywhere: in the breakers of the two oceans to either side of us, high on the mountain slopes that surrounded us, and strung out along the river that spilled from Kambalnoye Lake. But we had a big problem. These bears were all very afraid of us, and we caused stampedes wherever we showed ourselves. This reaction was certainly not what we had hoped for, but we had already committed ourselves to seeing this project through, in Kamchatka. We had to start the process of forming some kind of rapport with the hundreds of bears, no matter how shakily our relationship with them had begun.

On the bright side, Igor Revenko gave us encouraging news. The price of gall in China

Volcanic pumice is easily carved by wind and water, and is as light as balsa wood. We've watched large pieces float down rivers to the sea.

The sockeye at Kurilskoy Lake are so numerous
that bears will just sit and watch them—until they finally
become hungry enough to eat again.

Thinking that we may have caught a salmon right under
his nose, a lanky male stands up for a better view. Only his
ears have yet to shed their winter fur.

was dropping, and many poachers were turning to salmon fishing instead of killing bears. We hoped this change would be permanent.

Conventional thinking insists that bears that don't fear humans are inevitably dangerous, and to date most grizzlies that had decided to live near people had died for their transgressions. We had to show the world that this did not have to be the case, and in order to ensure a future for the grizzly, we had to do it soon. But in this respect, the first year of our study had been a failure. Much of what we wanted to understand depended on living among bears that were not afraid to explore a relationship with humans. With so many still afraid of us, it was clearly going to take a long time to earn the trust of a meaningful number of bears.

Heading home to Canada at the end of our first season, we knew that we had to find a new approach, so we stopped in Petropavlovsk to make a request of the Director of Preserves. Every year there were cubs orphaned by hunters and poachers, and the zoo was where they ended up, entertaining people until they outgrew their cages and were killed. We asked that the following spring we be allowed to take any available cubs to our cabin, to be reintroduced into the wild. To our surprise, the director was open to the idea, so we spent the winter planning how to spend our second season as new parents. The prospect of raising cubs was exciting; if it happened, our learning about bears would accelerate tenfold, and if we were successful, it would be the first time grizzlies would make the transition from a zoo environment to being truly wild.

A mature female rests at the shore but remains alert to her surroundings. We named her Sitting Bear because that was how she spent much of her time, enjoying the view across the lake.

Irises will bloom from the middle of July and into October in areas where snow lingers.

Igor Revenko's cabin on the shore of Kurilskoy Lake. Kambalnoye Lake is twenty-five miles over the ridges to the south.

Kamchatka's severe winters with deep snow and cold winds are redeemed by the bounty of the summers. Bears' ability to sleep for six months makes it easy for them to thrive in the region.

When Maureen was working on a documentary about grizzlies in the Rocky Mountains of Alberta, she would go weeks without seeing a brown bear. In Kamchatka she could photograph fifty in a day.

A young Itelmen gathers mushrooms for drying. The Itelman were indigenous to the area around Kurilskoy Lake. Eventually they were forced to pay a tax of sable skins to Russian conquerors, so they moved north to forested areas.

It was not a perfect world for the bears of South Kamchatka Sanctuary. Poachers took advantage of world markets to supplement their meagre incomes by killing bears for their gallbladders, which are sold into Southeast Asia as a traditional stomach medicine.

An Itelmen hunter's bag, displaying eagle feathers and a wolf skull.

The big males spend most of their time at the river. A bear will even sleep all night on a favourite perch, so as not to have to reclaim it the next day.

In September, brown bears will cease fishing
for a week or more to disappear into the pines
to eat nuts. Some Kamchatkan bears never eat salmon;
all of them eat pine nuts.

Bears have several ways of removing nuts from cones.
This female is using her tongue to roll the cone around in her
mouth until the nuts fall out. She then spits out the husk like
a wad of chewing tobacco, and breaks the nuts with her teeth
so they can be digested more quickly.

During the first year of our study, it was very discouraging to have bears constantly flee our presence.
This female has four cubs, which is quite common, although three is the norm.

Mature males weigh between one thousand and fifteen hundred pounds, and can look very menacing.
Although some of the males make a practice of killing and eating cubs, those predator bears have never threatened us.

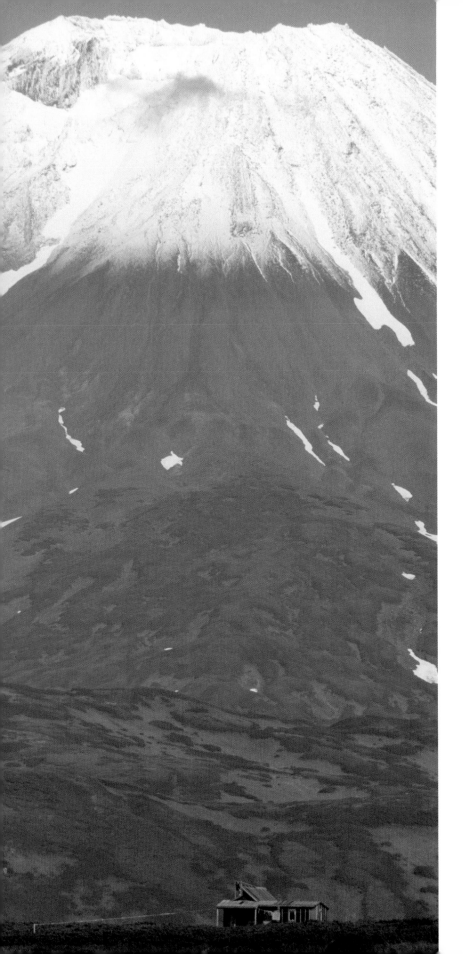

We built our cabin in just three weeks;
violent storms had made it impossible to stay in a tent.

The cabin, as seen from Kambalnoye Lake.

Kambalnoye River is a conduit for the sockeye salmon that spawn in the lake.
To complete their journey they have to survive a gauntlet of as many as 125 bears.

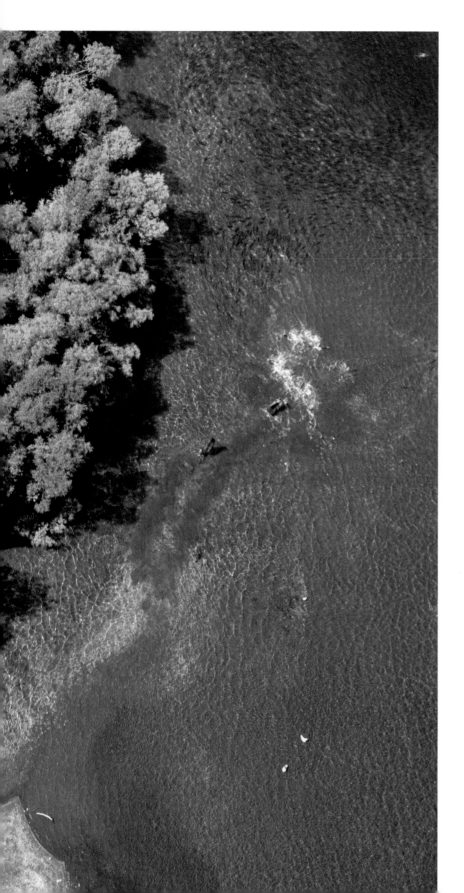

We rarely have visitors, but when we do, they always come by helicopter.

Built by Charlie in 1992, the Kolb has worked in the wilderness without technical support for ten years.

From the Kolb, we could photograph bears (and salmon!) from directly overhead. Usually the bears paid no attention.

The valley surrounding Kambalnoye Lake has been home ground for seven years. Our cabin is a white dot on the left (circled).

Gorelaya Volcano. As seen from the air, its lake appears turquoise, due to its chlorine and sulfur content.

A bear fishes in the Sea of Okhotsk, at the mouth of a spawning stream. The 7000-foot volcano in the background makes up one island in the long string of Kuril Islands.

A smouldering Mutnovskiy Volcano, located along the flight path between Petropavlovsk and Kambalnoye Lake.

One of the two lakes in the Ksudach Volcano crater.

The skeleton of a blue whale, recently picked clean by bears. Within one year, storms would clear away everything except a couple of vertebrae. The whale skull was seventeen feet long.

A trail made only by bears.

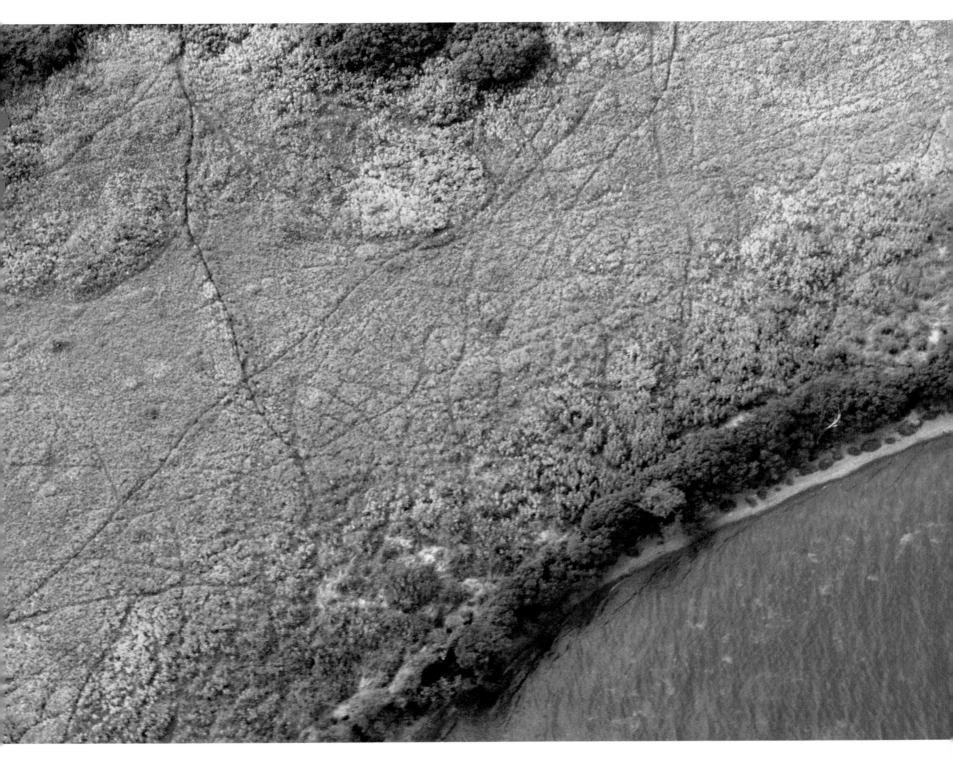

Bear trails through the brush. Some have been worn into the
hard ground a foot deep from centuries of use.

Our First Year with the Cubs—1997

Returning to Kamchatka in early May of 1997, we learned that there were three young female cubs who had recently been placed in a zoo after their mother was killed by a hunter. We were ecstatic at the chance to be their guardians; however, our request for orphaned cubs seemed to have been long forgotten. But one look at the cubs and the deplorable condition of the zoo was all it took to fix our resolve. After a great deal of negotiating—and a little bending of the rules—the cubs were lifted free of their cage to come with us to Kambalnoye Lake.

What followed was the launch of our cub reintroduction project, and a summer that we will always remember as the happiest time of our lives. Instead of us being parents to these three young bears, it was more as if they taught us how to be children again. Their joy for life was contagious, and through their eyes and their experiences we were finally able to enter into the world of bears—a world in which human presence was not only tolerated but accepted as a natural part of daily life.

Naming the cubs Chico, Biscuit and Rosie, we set about creating a home for them at Kambalnoye. We built them a small cabin for shelter, within a large pen surrounded by electric fencing, making sure they had alders to climb and soft earth in which to dig. The precaution of the pen was necessary, because small cubs roaming on their own would be vulnerable to any predator bears in the area. At first we were afraid to let the cubs out at all, as if even the vastness of the land could swallow them up, but our fears soon proved unfounded. Though delighted with their new freedoms, the cubs stuck close to us, often running in big circles while keeping us at the centre.

When the cubs had adjusted to their new home and learned to come when we called or whistled, we began to introduce them to the rest of the basin. Each day, we took Chico, Biscuit and Rosie on long walks into the rich wilderness that surrounded the cabin, trying to

It didn't take Chico long to climb the door of her new cabin and find the narrow gap we'd dismissed as too small for a cub to fit through.

impress upon them our wisdom and our knowledge of what they should be eating. Within the pen they were fed twice a day—at first porridge with lots of milk, then, as they got older, shelled sunflower seeds. But we were determined to expose them to the proper natural food sources as well. Right from the start, however, they were much quicker than we were in figuring out what was nutritious and what would give them a bellyache. Most important, though, we taught them how to catch fish, two years sooner than they would have learned with their mother. This skill would be crucial to their survival, because in the fall we would be gone and the cubs would be on their own.

Observant bears around the valley seemed surprised by what they were seeing: the odd-looking creatures who walked on their hind legs now had cubs of their own, and were protecting them. Soon, many other bears besides our cubs were accepting our presence.

But we also wanted to find out whether human-bear relations could ever be free of the fear of physical harm. We had been careful to set strict limits with the cubs, but of the three, Chico wanted most to play with us. We decided to allow physical contact with her only, as long her playfulness with us was gentle, to see how such a relationship would change over time.

By fall, we were letting Chico, Biscuit and Rosie leave their pen whenever they chose—but as they were thriving, we were filled with anxiety. To our relief, the cubs learned to protect themselves by climbing cliffs, where the big bears did not have the agility to follow. But would they know how to find a place to sleep for the whole winter? The cubs didn't seem worried; in fact, the cooler the days got, the happier they seemed. Successful hibernation depended on the cubs gaining large amounts of fat, so they kept busy consuming the plentiful pine nuts and salmon in the area. By October the cubs were round with thick new fur, and would spend several days away without us knowing where they had gone. We imagined they might be scouting for a place to den.

By November 8, we had a few inches of snow, the lake was freezing over and the barometer and the sky indicated a huge storm brewing. The three cubs slowly climbed over a ridge, stopping to play as though it were a hot summer's day, then disappeared into the swirling storm. It was the last we saw of them for six months.

Chico dug a hole in the snow and then tried to pull the roof down on herself.

Our fears that the young cubs would escape our protective watch were eased when we realized that their new games centred on us. The cubs would run away but come back at high speed, run circles around us until they were puffing, and then pile up in a heap of teeth and fur.

For the cubs, the first few weeks in their new home was a time of constant discovery and fun, but they also seemed to understand the need to be careful.

The cubs' travel box (their halfway house between the zoo and freedom) was cramped, but their quiet, watchful patience seemed to indicate they knew there were exciting adventures ahead.

The cubs were always entertaining, and their joy infected us as well.

Rosie.

Chico, trying to be patient, waits in her bowl to be fed.

Each day, the cubs repeated their cycle of hard play and sleep. At this age bears have two speeds: full throttle ahead and complete stop.

Chico, Biscuit and Rosie all loved the water, and the excitement it added to their games. Our daily walks often took the form of pool-hopping.

Rarely were the cubs out of sight of each other for more than a few seconds,
and they usually slept in a pile. For one nap, Chico was a convenient pillow.

As they discovered edible and nutritious plants in the area, the cubs began to push for more independence.
They'd always come when we whistled for them, but often seemed to wonder what all the fuss was about.

An electric fence kept the cubs safe from predator males.

As Chico, Biscuit and Rosie got bigger, they
only sought the shelter of the cabin during extreme storms,
but they did sometimes use it for play. Here they seem to be
waiting for Goldilocks to drop by.

In order to teach the cubs how to fish, Charlie would catch a tub full of trout and put them in a shallow, contained pool, where they could be caught more easily. Below, Charlie and biologist Igor Revenko urge Chico on.

Chico displays remarkable patience waiting for her fish, which I tossed to shore for her to eat. The very tricky responsibility of feeding the cubs without them becoming aggressive later was possible only because we never fed them anything by hand.

It takes a bit of nerve to swim naked with a grizzly bear, but it was the bears' capacity for trust that Charlie wanted to understand.

We gradually introduced the cubs to their wider surroundings. Here, Maureen shows the cubs new territory across the bay.

The cubs were always alert to the presence of other bears. At this age, their fear would send them into panicked flight.

It's a humbling experience to recognize the intelligence bears
display in their awareness of their natural surroundings.

The main focus of our work with the cubs and with all of the bears in the area was trust. We worked with Chico in particular to explore the limits of human-bear interaction—limits that were to be tested with her only. In one game, Charlie would grab a handful of fur between Chico's ears and she would place her claws on his hand and slowly begin to apply pressure, until he had to let go.

Having learned that she was allowed to touch us, Chico enjoyed what to her must have seemed a special advantage.

Our daily walks with the cubs took on the feeling of supreme privilege for us, and were not the mundane chore
the word rehabilitation might imply. It was never clear: were we the givers or the receivers?

By September, the cubs were in beautiful condition.
They would soon be fat enough to den successfully—providing they could figure out how.

In order to study their ways of communicating,
Maureen recorded the many subtle sounds bears make.

One particular section of lakeshore was a bountiful
place to find salmon and also offered a quick route to
the grassy cliffs above the lake, where the big bears
could not pursue the cubs.

Biscuit and Rosie in early fall.

In early September, crowberries were more
than just dessert—they were important food.

For bears, the right kind of mud can provide pure bliss—
it not only cools down their fur, but keeps biting flies at bay.

Chico.

Accustomed to getting up with us for their pre-dawn feedings, the cubs rose earlier
than other bears, and always enjoyed having the shore to themselves.

Chico could make herself comfortable anywhere.

The problem with having a hard and fast rule against looking a bear in the eye is that you miss
seeing the intelligence there, and love—and perhaps their kind-hearted pity for your human limitations.

Biscuit on the lookout for danger.

October was a time for lassitude. By then, the cubs had grown from
their spring weight of 10 pounds to a solid 100 pounds, and were almost ready for hibernation.

With snow on the ground and the lake frozen, denning-time was not far off.

The mountains surrounding the Kambalnoye basin were still deep in snow when we returned in early May of 1998. It had been a strange winter for us: thousands of miles away from the three extraordinary animals we had grown so attached to, envisioning them snuggled together in a den, and hoping they were safe, comfortable and content.

We had never doubted that the cubs would remember us, but their response to our return was even more than we had hoped for: seeing them for the first time, it was as if we had only been away for a few days. Chico, Biscuit and Rosie ran down the mountain to greet us, bounding and sliding like the fun-loving

youngsters we had left behind. All three cubs rubbed their faces in our scent in the snow. But then Chico lay on her back, put her paw up and meshed her claws with Charlie's fingers. So began the second year of trying to understand the makeup of our very special kinship.

We never did find out where our cubs denned that first winter, but they had clearly taken it all in stride, despite having to figure it out on their own. They also had a new air of maturity about them, one that we did not see in other cubs their age, who would still be with their mothers. That snowy May, most of the Kambalnoye females took their cubs to the east coast, where spring was usually a month

After six months of living on their own, the orphaned cubs immediately rolled around in Charlie's tracks. Judging by their sun-bleached fur, we estimated they had denned for five and a half months and re-emerged three weeks before our arrival.

Three sets of yearling tracks near the cabin were the first signs we had that the cubs had survived the winter.

ahead of the higher country and food sources were opening up. But until the snow finally melted from the mountainsides and herbs became available, Chico, Biscuit and Rosie survived on pine nuts left over from the previous season and a few fish they found frozen in the lake ice.

Another sign of the cubs' self-reliance was that they didn't look to us to protect them from a very dangerous large male in the area, who made a habit of killing and eating young bears. (It seems that in areas where bear numbers are high, there's usually one of these cannibals around.) The cubs spent nights on a small ledge high on a cliff, and during the day outran the big bear if he made a move on them. It was nerve-racking for us to watch them, especially on the occasions they only escaped by inches. As much as we wished we could interfere, survival was up to the cubs now.

We continued to have wonderful times with the cubs, but they were now unquestionably a part of the wild-bear community. Their territory was about ten square miles, but they would occasionally invite us to travel with them. In passing, they would lope up to the cabin—their arrival

With good footing on hard snow, and some supplemental feed from us, our yearling orphans could outrun the adult male that preyed on cubs at Kambalnoye Lake.

sounded like a herd of horses coming through—and stop at the fence. If we made any move towards getting ready to come, they would wait. If not, they would pound off again and disappear.

Accompanying them was always an awe-inspiring expedition into the world they now regarded as theirs. We travelled with them not as substitute parents, but as close observers of how wild bears lived. They were not afraid of humans, which defies conventional notions of wildness, but such restrictive definitions are best reserved for people who need to see themselves as separate from the natural world. In terms of freedom and self-sufficiency, our cubs had taken their rightful places in the Kamchatkan wild.

Of course, we were also still exploring the nature of our shared trust, and Chico still loved

to have the mosquitoes brushed away from around her eyes while she napped. The praise she received for a great catch of a leaping trout or salmon seemed to cement our bond with her, because it indicated our interest in what she was doing. Understanding her reactions meant understanding the most important and remarkably simple key to having a way with animals: recognizing what we share in intelligence, feelings and emotions.

Every other year, pink salmon spawn upstream from the cabin, in Char Creek. The cubs' second season in Kamchatka, in 1998, coincided with this bounty of protein and fat. It gave them the opportunity to hone their fishing skills and to fatten up in preparation for their second winter. Before the cubs denned that year, however, Rosie must have made a terrible mistake—one that

The bears had little to eat in the spring, and we were surprised by how they could survive on their fat from the previous year. Supplemented with vegetation as it became available, this fat would keep them going until salmon showed up in mid-August.

No privacy, even in the privy.

caused her to be caught and killed by the predator bear. We had gone home by then, and didn't know of her fate until we saw she was missing the next spring. We eventually found where the big bear had buried her remains, and DNA analysis later confirmed that we had found Rosie. A deep sadness hung over us all that summer, but we also realized that the risks Rosie faced were an integral part of her freedom and inseparable from the pleasures of her life.

By the middle of our 1999 season, we realized we had an opportunity with our study that would probably never be repeated: the chance to determine whether the trust we had established with Chico and Biscuit and the other bears who lived near our cabin was sustainable. This meant being with them for hundreds of hours, trying to learn everything we could about their habits, preferences and reactions. It was clear by now that not only our cubs but other grizzlies remembered us year to year, and accepted our presence at Kambalnoye Lake, but we needed to know exactly how far that acceptance went.

In dealing with most of the bears in the area, we simply learned how not to interfere with their obtaining of food. With Chico and Biscuit, however, we hoped we could unravel the reason why bear-human relations almost invariably turn sour. We worked out ways to help them whenever we could, hoping all the time not to step too far over a boundary we didn't fully understand. They would pick up on our intentions when we asked them to follow us to an extra good place to fish, or if we signalled the presence of a dead salmon by splashing a rock into the water beside it. At other times, we let them know we simply wanted to go along on walks to observe what they were doing, with nothing but companionship on offer. As long as we did not get in the way and never played tricks that would make them look foolish, our positive relationship deepened. Showing them where to find fish was a wildcard we played with to

speed up our understanding of the fine line between being helpful and being seen as providers.

But we also sometimes crossed that line intentionally, in order to learn what might happen. For a short time that summer, Charlie would collect salmon and hand them directly to Biscuit. This quickly created uncomfortable expectations, and whenever she saw us she'd come running to see what we had for her. We were very worried about her reaction, but we found that when we stopped feeding her this way, her unrealistic and potentially dangerous expectation that we would fish for her went away within a day. We are often trying to accelerate our learning process, and sometimes these kinds of tests are necessary, but so far all potentially negative changes in Biscuit's behaviour have been easy to rectify.

Time out for a lazy researcher and his lazy subjects.

As spring progressed and the lake began to open up, the cubs occasionally found fish that had been frozen in the ice the previous fall.

In late June, salamanders lay their eggs on stems of grass along the edges of the small lakes north of the cabin.

Unfortunately for the salamanders, Biscuit developed quite a taste for the eggs.

Rosie caught on quickly.

Maureen films mist lifting off the lake, seemingly oblivious to the grizzly
eating a salmon four feet to her right. Mornings along the lakeshore could be wonderfully nonchalant.

From an early age, Chico came across as a ham.

The cubs eventually learned how to judge other bears' intentions towards them.

By our second year, the cubs were displaying increasing degrees of independence.
We would often hear them gallop up to the cabin and stop. If we picked up our gear, they would wait for us to come
and spend the day with them. If we made no move to get up, they would head out to explore on their own.

Biscuit and Maureen.

Charlie tries not to disturb the peaceful atmosphere as he flies past to see what Maureen and the bears are doing.

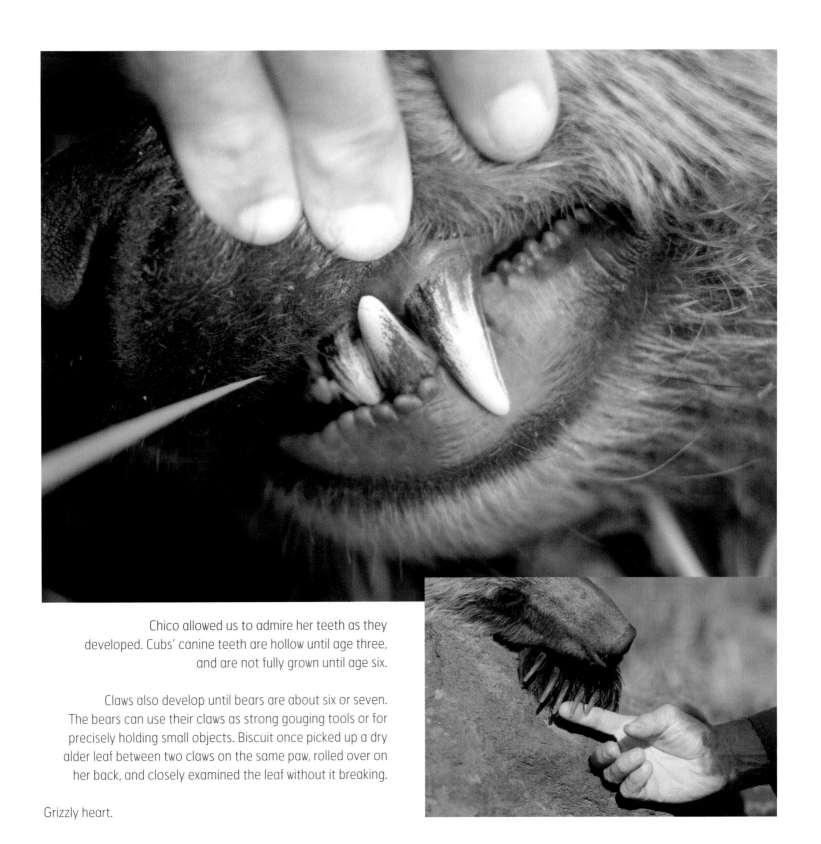

Chico allowed us to admire her teeth as they developed. Cubs' canine teeth are hollow until age three, and are not fully grown until age six.

Claws also develop until bears are about six or seven. The bears can use their claws as strong gouging tools or for precisely holding small objects. Biscuit once picked up a dry alder leaf between two claws on the same paw, rolled over on her back, and closely examined the leaf without it breaking.

Grizzly heart.

Chico at the lakeshore, late summer.

It required us looking through binoculars to see what Chico and Biscuit could
smell easily: a bear on the opposite shore, a thousand yards away.

Patches of snow frame the lush greenery of Kambalnoye basin well into July.

Early summer is a time of quiet contentedness, before the urgency of
having to get fat for hibernation sets in. By August, bears take on serious dispositions.

Chico glances back at us, looking for praise of her spectacular catch of a pink salmon.

The first of many salmon to be amazed—too late—by Biscuit's fishing prowess.
By the second fall the cubs displayed remarkable skill, and were even able to fish the river.

Biscuit, at two years and seven months of age.

Edenic existence is an attainable goal for those who understand the
appropriate courtesies of living in the wilderness—most importantly kindness, attention, and respect.

Strong and Independent 2000-2002

By 2000, Chico and Biscuit were very much on their own. We were still inquisitive and pried into their lives, but it had been a couple of years since we had been important to their survival—other than indirectly, by funding the ranger protection program. After our initial good-will gesture of taking the cubs from the zoo and giving them an opportunity to become independent, they continued to accept us with total trust. That has never changed. And as a result of this closeness, we have been able to sense even the most subtle nuances of frustration or satisfaction in the cubs, and their annual shifts in behaviour when they needed to apply themselves to the task of getting fat enough to survive the long winter ahead. We can now clearly recognize these mood changes, as well as observe how these reintroduced animals live on the land with other bears.

There are things we have comprehended from this closeness that we could not have resolved otherwise. For instance, accidentally doing things that we know are mistakes does not spell trouble with a grizzly—as long as trust has been established previously. Whether it is them scaring us or the other way around (both humans and bears are prone to slipping and falling on steep hillsides!), it is quickly understood as an accident. We've also established that bears are often solitary not because they really prefer to be, but because they need to spread out widely when food is scarce so they don't have to compete for every mouthful.

Now we are combining our individual skills to help us tell the world what we have learned about bears. Both of us take slides to illustrate our books, but Maureen, with her painting and sculpting, works to appeal to people through intuitive awareness. Her quest over the years has been to learn to fit in with and become part of nature, comfortably exploring the tundra and the waterways with bears on their terms. One sculpture, titled *Into the Deep: A Path of Entry*, used cement tablets that contained castings of many different bear tracks found in the mud where lakes dried up in the summer. Symbolic of emotional and physical entry into a bear's

Biscuit.

world, the piece gives viewers a glimpse of what it could be like to live in a world in which bears and humans peacefully shared the same land.

Maureen also became convinced that bears could appreciate beauty, and that the places bears have carved out for many years high on mountainsides are located purposely where they can enjoy the scenery. These "nesting sites," as Maureen terms them, are not just favourite sleeping spots, but so much more. She has spent many hours in these ancient beds herself, looking out at bears' eye level, creating paintings about what and how bears see. These paintings have been exhibited in Moscow. A photo in the entrance to the show, showing Maureen surrounded by the cubs as she painted, had the caption "As it was in the beginning," implying that if humankind hadn't insisted on dominance, our relationship with wild animals could have turned out quite differently.

In late August of 2000, Chico left the Kambalnoye Lake basin. At the time there were lots of spawning salmon available, but some bears get bored eating nothing but salmon, and many had departed to various parts of the Kambalnoye drainage basin in search of other foods. Having decided at the outset that we would not inconvenience the bears with heavy radio collars, where Chico went is one of those mysteries we can only hope to sort out over time.

Since Chico left the basin, Biscuit has made Kambalnoye her home territory. While she shares the area with several bears, a bear we call Brandy is the only other female who lives full time around the lake. Watching over the years how bears disperse, it seems unlikely Chico and Biscuit could have settled in the same area. And considering how cranky Brandy is with her kind, Biscuit has had to be very confident to fit into the same domain.

Brandy has become very important to our study, and has raised two sets of cubs close to our cabin. She has given us much insight into mother grizzlies—often touted as the most dangerous animals a person could happen upon. Brandy is startlingly ferocious with male bears she thinks could menace her cubs, but she recognized early on that we were not a threat. Her trust in us is so complete that she will even leave her cubs with us while she runs another bear intruder out of the valley. This behaviour reaffirms how

It was thrilling to come back each year and find our tiny orphan cubs developing into strong, independent bears who were confident in their surroundings.

important trust is to brown bears, and makes us wonder if harassment with rubber bullets, among other things, might be why the female grizzlies in our mountain parks are so inclined to turn on people in defence of their cubs.

After being immersed in our work for seven years, we are becoming increasingly confident in saying that a grizzly bear's nature is to be peaceful towards humans, and that bears will accept human presence if they are not mal-treated. There are, of course, many dos and don'ts in getting along [see page 151], but we hope that our research has shown that by pay-ing attention to certain protocols, people can one day learn to coexist with grizzles.

South Kamchatka Sanctuary was created to protect salmon and bears, and it appears to be doing so, to a large degree. We are determined to ensure that South Kamchatka remains the sanctu-ary it was intended to be, and continue our efforts in maintaining this understanding with the Russian government. Even after our study at Kambalnoye Lake winds down, we will watch carefully to see that the ranger program continues to get funding, so that all of the bears—and the salmon they rely on—can continue to prosper.

At the time of our departure at the end of the 2002 season, Biscuit was thriving. At what we guessed was five hundred pounds, she had even grown larger than Brandy, despite being half her age. And in June of 2002, we saw her being bred by two large, differently coloured males, several days apart. If all goes well, Biscuit will have had cubs of varying hues in January 2003. The event will carry with it a wonderful sense of achievement for us. It is rare that one succeeds in reintroducing a bear to the wild, let alone has the opportunity to follow the results over a number of successive years. And although Biscuit was initially brought up by us, we're sure she well understands that there are ill-intentioned bears in her world that she might have to over-power in order to successfully raise her cubs to the position of strength and independence she herself enjoys. There is a good chance this will happen even on this first, most vulnerable, attempt to raise cubs. Successful parenthood is a learned skill in bears as well as in humans. Biscuit's size and intelligence should give her the advantage she will need to be a great mother, which will ensure the genes she shared with Chico and Rosie will become a permanent legacy to Kambalnoye Lake.

As soon as their stomachs were full, Chico and Biscuit would play like little cubs.

As the years passed, walking with the bears became even more of an impressive undertaking, due to their size.

Each spring, after not having seen each other all winter, Chico and Charlie had their special greeting.

Snow often made Biscuit feel playful. She would leap into the water, leap out again, then run around us in circles—just as the cubs had done so many times in our first year.

Worried that poachers might be in the area, Charlie wanted to check for bullet holes in the bear skull Chico had found. At first Chico was protective of her find, but then she decided to look the other way. Once Charlie confirmed there weren't any holes, he gave back the skull.

Our bears' favourite place to pursue pink salmon was a place we called Char Creek, which ran through a beautiful canyon north of our cabin. Pink salmon spawned in Char Creek only in years with even numbers.

The final leap.

Biscuit's turn to show off.

It was a wonderful privilege be a witness to the bears playing.

Chico and Biscuit matured quickly, but until they became fully confident
around other bears, the cliff above Bear Skull Bay was their well-protected hangout.

Biscuit's face frequently changes with her feelings. Here she's about to be pounced upon by Chico.

While Charlie continued to puzzle over the troubled psychology of human-bear relationships, Maureen persevered in making controversial statements through her art.

Grizzly tracks inspired Maureen to create a piece that would take the viewers into the bears' world. She cast several dozen in plaster and carried them back home to Alberta. In her studio, Maureen completed her work with a series of 2 x 2–foot concrete tablets, each weighing a hundred pounds. She called the finished piece *Into the Deep: A Path of Entry.*

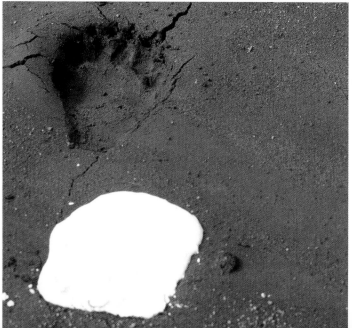

The strong colours of the spawned-out salmon greatly influenced many of Maureen's paintings.

Oversight, Maureen's charcoal drawing of Brandy, Lemon and Lime.

Our last photograph of Chico (right), still the darker of the two,
before she departed the Kambalnoye Lake basin for parts unknown.

Salmon would spawn, die, and sink to the bottom of the shallow
bay. Biscuit gathered them up with her feet. She would bring the
fish to the surface, toss them into the air, then catch and eat them.

Charlie takes a stroll with Brandy and her two yearlings, Gin and Tonic. One of the most
important things the bears of Kambalnoye Lake have taught us is that humans don't have to be
misfits in the bear world—that you can fit in as long as you don't make a nuisance of yourself.

Brandy, Gin and Tonic.

Gin at age three, a year after he was weaned.

Brandy's summer off between cub litters. Not having to nurse,
she focused her attention on the bounty of Char Creek and quickly put on fat.

Gin sometimes travels behind Charlie—and Brandy doesn't mind.

The look on a bear's face can be deceptive. This bear hung out around
the cabin all one fall, and although he looked fierce, he was actually very easy to get along with.

Walking along the lakeshore, we came upon Brandy nursing her second pair of cubs, Lemon and Lime. She was clearly comfortable in our presence, as she allowed us to proceed around her, along the narrow shore. She didn't even look up as we passed by.

Walnut is another of the resident bears we see year after year, but he always waits until the middle of August to show up.

Brandy didn't even mind letting us have a close-up of her suckling her cubs.

Brandy occasionally startled us with a sudden loud hiss if we got in her way, but her roaring ferociousness with other bears made our hair stand on end.

Brandy would get Lemon and Lime playing, then leave them with us to frolic.

By the summer of 2002 Biscuit stood eight feet tall, and weighed about 500 pounds.

Year after year we have lived with several generations of bears who do not fear humans.
From our experiences we have grown to know the joys of being a part of their world.

Biscuit relaxes after circumnavigating Kambalnoye Lake in search of spawning salmon.

Maureen babysitting Lemon.

Lime sits still and holds her paw up at different angles. She looks like a child waiting for the teacher to call on her.

Biscuit and Charlie have a lakeside chat about trust and what it means in terms of world affairs.

When shaking hands with an animal with a reputation as nefarious as the grizzly's, the tender finesse of the grip can be surprising.

Within three months of this photo being taken, we expect that Biscuit will have had her own cubs while snug in her den under the snow, sometime in January 2003.

Biscuit.

A Protocol for Co-existence
between Grizzlies and Humans

• Use electric fencing to keep bears out of where people live and away from toilets, garbage, and anything else bears could eat or damage.

• Always assume that bears' activity is important to them and do your best not to interfere, especially when their need to fatten becomes urgent in late summer and fall. Staying out of bears' way is always the most important thing.

• In surprise encounters, talk to bears, calmly.

• Always carry pepper spray in bear country, to be used only at close range in dangerous encounters.

• Play dead only when you have forgotten your pepper spray, when talking to them has failed and when you know you are a couple of bounds away from being knocked down by a grizzly. (And remember, never play dead with a black bear.)

• A little harder to learn, but very enjoyable for anybody with a love of wild animals, is to appreciate the intelligence, instincts, vulnerabilities and memory of bears. If you want to go into bear country, you should be willing to learn that too.

• If you live in bear country (which can be a village or the edge of a big city), bears will periodically come calling. Don't automatically assume that this situation is dangerous. Leave the bear at peace and make sure you and your neighbours keep all attractants where bears cannot get into them. Meet as a group with your neighbours and the local officials in charge of these matters. Then, as a team, decide whether you want to attempt to live with the bears or not. There is more information available all the time on living with bears, but if you decide not to do so, bears can be encouraged to go elsewhere without having to kill or even transport them. Make sure your officials know how to do this, and, if need be, help research the necessary information.

Acknowledgements

Ideas by themselves do not ripen into achievement without funding. We have depended on foundations and corporations who believed in what we were attempting to do. Their financial support and encouragement have made our work with grizzlies possible and we continue to appreciate their much-needed assistance.

We thank the following organizations: The Schad Foundation, who have most generously supported our work from day one, Clayoquot Island Preserve, Fanwood Foundation West, Parallax Film Productions Inc., Raincoast Conservation Foundation, Craighead Environmental Research Institute, Masters Gallery Ltd., Sun Microsystems Ltd. of both Canada and the United States, Mogens F. Smed Fund of the Calgary Foundation, Smed International Ltd., Peter Bush Foundation, the Alberta Foundation for the Arts, the Canada Council, Daymen Photo Marketing Ltd., Lowe Pro U.S.A. Inc., Counter Assault, Big Rock Brewery Ltd., the Great Bear Foundation, Trail of the Great Bear Society, S. M. Blair Family Foundation, Kodak Canada Inc., Development Matters Inc., Ralph Heddin Associates Ltd., Dr. J.V. Horsely Professional Corporation, Morton H. Wynne Insurance Agency Ltd., Canada Trust Mortgage Company, Conex Management Ltd., WSG Benefit Consultants Ltd., the Lynchpin Foundation, Microsoft Corporation, Trimac Corporation, the Calgary Zoo, and a foundation that wishes to remain anonymous.

Besides the corporate donors, the following individuals were generous with their friendship, time, and money. We are grateful for assistance from Robert and Birgit Bateman, Susan Bloom, Carol A. Bowker, Tom Ellison and Jenny Broom, Roland Dixon, James Gosling, Lynne and Rick Grafton, Rod and Lois Greene, Faith Hall, Mike and Maureen Heffring, Gayadel Heimbecker, N. J. Hewitt, Dr. Margaret Horne, Pat and Rosemarie Keough, Joan A. Martin, Peter McCombs and Debbie Conrad, Russ McKinnon, Uwe Mummenhoff, John and Barbara Poole, Anne, Peter and Tim Raabe, Signa Reid, Joan and Jack Sherman, Nicki and Mogens Smed, Ellen Smith, Neil Smith, Bert Van

Bekkum, Anthony Webb, Doug Williams, Gerry Zyphers, and approximately 350 others who either contributed items or made purchases at auction fundraisers.

The support of friends has come in many forms. For nine years we have relied on dozens of people around the world to make it possible to keep going on this long, drawn-out project. We are grateful for the support of Pamela Banting, Nancy Barrios, Walter Bovich, Esther and Michael Brenner, Lance Craighead, Al Crane, Creative Travel Adventures/Ried Morrison, DLS Imaging/Jo Cookson, Wendy Dudley, Rick and Bev Durvin, Ernest Enns and Lynne Woodworth, Pat and Joe Erickson, Bristol Foster, Hal Grainer, Valerie Haig-Brown, Frank Hall, Dr. Bill Hanlon, Nancy Hauser, LeeAnne Havens, Ian Herring, Jeanne Kaufman, Pat Klinck, Helen Kovaks, Bill and Tip Leacock, Matevz Lenarcic, Nik Lopoukhine, Anne Lukey, Sid Marty, Michael Mayzel, Ian and Karen McAllister, Debbie and Tim McDonald, Tom and Elaine McFadden, Mike McIntosh, Kathleen McNally, Linda and Ed McNally, Jeannie Minchin, Pat and Baiba Morrow, Doug Murray, Sybil Palmer, Peter and Nan Poole, Matt Read, Ursula and Rick Reynolds, Andy Russell, Dick Russell, Gordon Russell, John Russell, Selena Ronnquist, Clint Scherger, Myrna Shapter, Larry and Christine Smith, Ewa Sniatycka, Reno Sommerhalder, Hopie and Bob Stevens, Tom Sullivan, David Suzuki, Dave Taylor, Jan Theunisz, Rob Walker, and David Wilkie.

Friends in Russia who have made us feel welcome and helped us to achieve our goals are Fedia Farberov, Elena Gaisina, Tatiana and Vladimir Gordienko, Allison Grant, Valery Komerov, Viktor Komerov, Anatoly Kovolenkov, Martha Madsen, Alexey Maslov and Ekaterina Lepskaya, Vladimir Mosolov, Jennya Ptichkina and her family, Igor and Irina Revenko, Irina Viter, Olga Yefimova, and my remarkable pilot friends: Evgeny, Genna, Viktor, Vladimir, and Peter.

We thank the Canadian Embassy, Moscow, former Canadian ambassador Anne Leahy, and current Canadian ambassador Rodney Irwin for assisting us in presenting our work in Moscow.

The most important outcome of Maureen's and my work in Kamchatka was to be able to tell people about it: Maureen through her art, me through my writing, and both of us through our photographs. I am indebted to several people for making the book happen. My agent, Anne McDermid, introduced me to Anne Collins, of Random House Canada, who first published *Grizzly Heart,* our book that chronicles the more detailed story of our first five years in Russia. Without Fred Stenson's writing guidance, and his marvellous organizational and editorial skills, that book would not have read nearly as well as it does.

The success of *Grizzly Heart* in Canada made it seem natural to follow up with this volume, which enables us to relate the story of our project in a different way. Anne Collins, Pam Robertson and Pamela Murray assisted us in creating this book, and Gloria Goodman in Random House's rights department deserves our thanks as well. Sue Freestone, of Hutchinson in the UK, has been a very enthusiastic supporter of this project from the moment she learned of it. In addition, we are appreciative of Nigel Lang and Dawn Saunders-Dahl for the time they have spent scanning approximately 10,000 slides and building our database.

Another way that we have kept in touch with the world about our project is via our website (found at www.cloudline.org). Thanks to Paula Oswald for taking over as our webmaster after James Gosling set up the site and skilfully managed it for three years. Thanks as well to Barb Gosling and Derek Small for their friendship and for insisting we learn about computers.